Artists in Their Time

Pablo Picasso

Kate Scarborough

Franklin Watts
A Division of Scholastic Inc.
New York Toronto London Auckland Sydney
Mexico City   New Delhi   Hong Kong
Danbury, Connecticut

First published in 2002 by
Franklin Watts
96 Leonard Street
London EC2A 4XD

First American edition published
in 2002 by Franklin Watts
A Division of Scholastic Inc.
90 Sherman Turnpike
Danbury, CT 06816

Series Editor: Adrian Cole
Series Designer: Mo Choy
Art Director: Jonathan Hair
Picture Researchers: Diana Morris and Kathy Lockley

A CIP catalog record for this title
is available from the Library of Congress.

ISBN 0-531-12229-8 (Lib. Bdg.)
ISBN 0-531-16622-8 (Pbk.)

Printed in China

Acknowledgments

AA Photo Library: 32t. AKG London: 18b, 20bl © Succession Picasso/DACS 2002, 28b. Ancient Art & Architecture Collection: 14t. Archive Photos/Hulton Getty: fr cover bc & 29t. Photograph © 2002 The Art Institute of Chicago, All Rights Reserved: Gift of the Maymar Corporation, Mrs. Maurice Rothschild, Mr. & Mrs. Chauncey McCormick, Mary & Leigh Block Charitable Fund, Ada Turnbull Hertle Endowment, through prior gift of Mr. & Mrs. Edwin Hokin, 1954.270, 23 © Succession Picasso/DACS 2002. R. Belbin/Art Directors & Trip: 24t. British Museum, London: Bridgeman fr cover bl, 16t. Brooklyn Museum of Art, New York: Bridgeman 16bl. Burstein Collection/Corbis: 33 © Succession Picasso/DACS 2002. Central Press/Hulton Getty: 38t. Alvin Langdon Coburn/GEH/Hulton Archive: 43. Kieran Docherty/Reuters/Popperfoto: 41b. Fuji Television Gallery, Tokyo: 39 © Succession Picasso/DACS 2002. Harlingue-Viollet: 22t. Lipnitzki-Viollet: 30b, fr cover br & 35b. Courtesy of Lee Miller Archives: 6t, 20t, 22c, Lee Miller Archives 29b, 32c, 34, 36t. Moderna Museet, Stockholm: 19 © Succession Picasso/DACS 2002. James Morris/Axiom: 14bl. Musée National d'Art Moderne, Paris: AKG London 18t © ADAGP, Paris and DACS, London 2002, Artothek 31 © Succession Picasso/DACS 2002. Musée d'Orsay, Paris: Eric Lessing/AKG London 15t, Bridgeman 36b. Musée Picasso, Barcelona: MAS 11 © Succession Picasso/DACS 2002. Musée Picasso, Paris: Bridgeman 21 © Succession Picasso/DACS 2002, 25 © Succession Picasso/DACS 2002, 37 © Succession Picasso/DACS 2002. Museo Nacional Centro de Arte Reina Sofia, Madrid: Bridgeman 26 © Succession Picasso/DACS 2002. Museum of Fine Arts, Budapest: Eric Lessing/AKG London 12. Museum of Modern Art, New York: Lauros-Giraudon/Bridgeman: 17 © Succession Picasso/DACS 2002. By kind permission of the Penrose Estate, Sir Roland Penrose, Portrait of Picasso: 10, 24b. ND-Viollet: 15b. Chris Parker/Axiom: 40t. The Prado, Madrid: Bridgeman 8. Private Collection: Bridgeman 6bl. Pushkin Museum of Fine Arts, Moscow: Alexander Burkatowski/Corbis 13 © Succession Picasso/DACS 2002. Reuters/Popperfoto: 28t. Photo RMN-Michèle Bellot: 30t © Succession Picasso/DACS 2002, -Béatrice Hatala 35t © Succession Picasso/DACS 2002. D.Shaw/Axiom: 38c. Tate Gallery, London: fr cover c & 27 © Succession Picasso/DACS 2002. Vanni Archive/Corbis: 9b. Collection Viollet: 9t. Wakefield Museum and Galleries: 41t © Henry Moore Foundation 2002. Nik Wheeler/Corbis: 7t.

Whilst every attempt has been made to clear copyright
should there be any inadvertent omission please apply
in the first instance to the publisher regarding rectification.

Contents

Who Was Pablo Picasso?

Pablo Picasso is perhaps the most famous of all 20th century artists. During his lifetime, he created a large number of works of art – from paintings and sculptures, to ceramics and lithographs. His passion to experiment and his fearless use of different styles led to innovations that had a great impact on contemporary artists and made his name known throughout the world.

"When I was a child, my mother said to me, 'If you become a soldier, you'll be a general. If a monk, you'll end up as the Pope!' Instead, I became a painter and wound up as Picasso."

Pablo Picasso

▲ **Pablo Ruiz Picasso, age 15.**

▲ *Pigeons*, **José Ruiz Blasco, 1888.** Picasso later said his father's good, but not great, art was "for dining rooms."

DETERMINED TO DRAW

Pablo Ruiz Picasso was born on October 25, 1881. He was the first child of artist Don José Ruiz Blasco and his wife, María Picasso. It is said that before Pablo Picasso could walk he was already determined to copy his father and draw. He would cry for a "Piz! Piz!" meaning *lapiz*, which is the Spanish word for pencil.

Picasso's father, Don José, painted in a traditional style favored at the time and he particularly liked to depict birds. However, he sold little of his work. His small income came from working as a curator of the Málaga Museum and teaching art.

TIMELINE ▶

October 25, 1881	1884	1887	1888	1889	1891
Pablo Ruiz Picasso is born in Málaga, Spain. First son of José Ruiz Blasco and Maria Picasso y Lopez.	Birth of his sister Dolorès (better known as Lola).	Birth of his second sister Conceptión, or Conchita.	Encouraged by his father, Picasso starts to paint.	Picasso's first recorded painting, using oil on wood, of a bullfight – a subject he will return to.	The family move to La Coruña, in northern Spain. Conchita dies of diphtheria.

A NATURAL TALENT

Don José quickly recognized his young son's natural talent and started educating him in his studio at home. In 1889, Picasso, age 7, completed his first recorded picture: a Spanish picador at a bullfight.

In 1891, Don José accepted a job as professor of drawing in La Coruña in northern Spain. He and his family – his wife, son, and two younger daughters – moved 450 miles (725 km) north to the Atlantic coast. Here, Don José continued to encourage Picasso's painting. His son was already an accomplished artist, so his father began to let him complete the birds in his own pictures. One evening

▲ Fishing boats fill the harbor at La Coruña today, while cars fill the street alongside. It would have been equally busy when Picasso moved there, with a very different atmosphere to the sun-drenched Málaga he left behind.

he left Picasso to finish the legs on a pigeon. Don José was so moved by the final result that he handed his son his paintbrushes, saying that his son's talent was greater than his own. At the time, Picasso was only 13 years old.

MÁLAGA AND LA CORUÑA

Málaga, the town in which Picasso was born, is situated in southern Spain on the Mediterranean coast. The small town is centered around the port and, at the time, depended heavily on the income from fishing and farming. The surrounding land was cultivated for olives, lemons, and figs.

When Picasso's father accepted a job in La Coruña, it was a big step up in his career. La Coruña was one of Spain's largest ports and the art school was well-known. However, Don José took his family away from the warmth of the Mediterranean sun to the harsh, wind-swept coast of the Atlantic.

Learning His Craft

La Coruña was not a happy place for Picasso. His younger sister, Conchita, died tragically from diphtheria and his father was often depressed and homesick for Málaga. Picasso spent most of his time practicing his drawing skills. His father sent him to the local art school, where he was taught in the Classical style. He also drew and painted from life, including portraits of his surviving sister, Lola, and models hired by his father.

A VISIT TO MADRID

After four years, the family returned to the Mediterranean – to Barcelona where Don José had accepted a job as professor of drawing at the Academy of Fine Arts, better known as La Lonja.

▲ *Las Meninas (The Maids of Honor)*, **Diego Rodrigues de Silva y Velázquez, c.1656.** This picture hangs along with many other Velázquez in the Prado in Madrid. As a student, Picasso described Velázquez as "first class."

"My first drawings could never have been shown at an exhibition of children's drawings. I lacked the clumsiness of a child, his naivety. I made academic drawings from the age of seven, the minute precision of which frightened me."

Pablo Picasso

TIMELINE ▶

1892	1894	Spring 1895	July 1895	September 1895
Picasso joins the School of Fine Art where his father is teaching. His studies outside of art are poor.	Picasso writes and illustrates journals. He draws Classical statues in class.	Father accepts teaching post in Barcelona. The family moves there in the summer.	Picasso visits Madrid and the Prado museum for the first time.	Picasso accepted at La Lonja, the School of Fine Arts in Barcelona where his father teaches.

Before traveling to Barcelona, Picasso's family spent the summer in Málaga. On the way there, they stopped in Madrid and visited the Prado – Spain's national fine art museum. The experience was a revelation for the young artist – he was able to look at the works of great Spanish painters, such as El Greco, Goya, and Velázquez, for the first time.

A CHILD PRODIGY

In Barcelona, Picasso enrolled at La Lonja even though he was too young. The professors at the academy were astounded by his entrance examination. Picasso had finished the exercises the rest of the students took a month to do in a day. They called him a prodigy – a child with brilliant talents.

▲ The magnificent hall at the Academy of Fine Arts, La Lonja, Barcelona, where Picasso studied and his father taught. The art school followed the traditions of the past, training their pupils in Classical art.

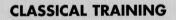

◀ A Roman statue of Venus, c. 150 B.C., held at the Prado, Madrid. As part of his training, Picasso had to draw copies of Classical sculptures such as this one.

CLASSICAL TRAINING

At the time Picasso was at art school, art was taught in the "Classical" tradition. The term referred back to the art of ancient Greece and Rome, whose ideas and styles had been rediscovered and developed during the European Renaissance about 1,000 years later. Classical art aspired to represent nature, including the human body, in its greatest beauty. From the Renaissance onward, the skills and techniques used in Classical art were formally taught, like a craft or science, in art schools throughout Europe. Picasso learned how to draw an object or paint a scene in accurate detail. He always believed this Classical training was essential in enabling him to realize his artistic vision.

Rites of Passage

▲ The interior of *Els Quatre Gats* at the end of the 19th century.

ELS QUATRE GATS

Els Quatre Gats was the meeting place of Barcelona's artists and writers – ideal for a young artist like Picasso looking for new inspiration and expression. Here he was able to discuss themes and methods that took him away from the Classical training he had acquired. The painters he met were influenced by Art Nouveau and the Impressionists. Picasso was able to take up their styles and imitate them successfully. Soon he became a leading member of the group and, in 1900, held his first exhibition there. Picasso made many friends at *Els Quatre Gats*, including another young artist, Carlos Casagemas, with whom he founded a studio.

Picasso's first major oil painting *The First Communion* (right) was completed when he was 15, and was exhibited in Barcelona in the spring of 1896. He chose to paint a scene familiar to every Catholic, a child's first holy communion, but he broke with tradition by showing the events before it – a hint, perhaps, of things to come.

AN END TO EDUCATION

In 1897, at age 16, Picasso was accepted into Madrid's Royal Academy of Art. His family pulled together to pay his fees, but he was still poor. Picasso relished the chance to spend more time in the Prado but disliked the teaching at the Academy. Much to his father's fury, he left after one term.

In the summer of 1898, Picasso traveled to a village called Horta de San Juan to stay with his friend, Manuel Pallarés.

Together they explored the rough and wild landscape and spent entire days painting. Picasso felt that the visit transformed him.

> *"All that I know, I learned in Pallarés village."*
>
> *Pablo Picasso*

◄ A street in Horta de San Juan. During his visit Picasso made many sketches of the village houses.

Back in Barcelona, Picasso began to establish himself with the city's intellectuals. He went regularly to *Els Quatre Gats* (The Four Cats) tavern, where Barcelona's artists gathered to discuss the latest ideas in art from all over Europe.

TIMELINE ▶

1896	June 1897	October 1897	Spring 1898	June 1898	1899
Picasso exhibits his first large-scale work, *The First Communion*.	Picasso's second big work, *Science and Charity*, given an honorable mention in a national exhibition of fine art.	Picasso starts at the Royal Academy in Madrid but leaves within months.	Picasso returns to Barcelona after having scarlet fever.	Picasso spends time with friend Pallarés in the village of Horta de San Juan.	Picasso begins to visit *Els Quatre Gats*. He meets, among others, artist Carlos Casagemas and poet Jaime Sabartés.

The First Communion, 1895-96

oil on canvas, 65 $\frac{1}{3}$ x 46 $\frac{2}{5}$ in (166 x 118 cm), Museo Picasso, Barcelona, Spain

Picasso constructed this painting according to his Classical training. However, he chose not to show the moment when the child receives communion, as would be expected of a traditional scene, but as she prepares for it. The altar boy is putting down a vase, a sign of movement, and not all the candles are lit.

Painting in Blue

In 1900, Picasso traveled to Paris with his friend Carlos Casagemas. It was a new and exciting environment for Picasso. The city was at the center of experimentation in art, which rejected Classical styles, a process begun by the Impressionists 40 years earlier. Picasso went back to Spain, his head filled with new ideas. Casagemas was less fortunate: he fell in love with an artist's model in Paris and, in the spring of 1901, killed himself when the affair ended unhappily.

The Annunciation, El Greco, 1600.
El Greco's choice of colors is similar to Picasso's during his Blue Period. His gaunt, elongated figures also influenced the young artist.

THE IMPACT OF TRAGEDY

His friend's suicide seemed to have a dramatic effect on Picasso's work. Over the next four years, many of his pictures were dominated by the color blue – his so-called "Blue Period."

Despite this, Picasso's art began to gain a wider audience. In June of 1901, he was given his first solo exhibition by Ambroise Vollard (1865-1939), an art dealer at the center of avant-garde art in Paris. It was not a huge success, but one critic wrote that Picasso was a "brilliant newcomer."

PICASSO'S BLUE PERIOD

The Old Jew With a Boy (right) was painted during the Blue Period (1901-04). Picasso said he chose to paint mainly in blue and grey because of his grief at the death of his friend Casagemas, but there may have been other reasons. Critics have suggested that Picasso only used blue paint because he bought a lot of it at a discounted price. Others have seen the influence of El Greco, who used similar cold tones. Whatever the reason, over the next four years, Picasso produced many somber images, featuring still, tragic characters – the poor and starving and social outcasts.

TIMELINE ▶

February 1900	October 1900	February 1901	May 1901	1902	1903
Picasso's first exhibition held at *Els Quatre Gats*.	Picasso and Casagemas travel to Paris. They return to Barcelona in December.	Casagemas commits suicide, shortly after returning to Paris.	Back in Paris, Picasso's Blue Period begins. He prepares for exhibition at Vollard's gallery.	Picasso moves between Barcelona and Paris, where he lives with poet Max Jacob.	Picasso is in Barcelona where he paints over 50 paintings in 14 months, including *La Vie* (Life).

The Old Jew With a Boy, 1903

oil on canvas, 49 ³/₅ x 36 ²/₃ in (126 x 93 cm), Pushkin Museum of Fine Arts, Moscow, Russia

The elongated limbs of the old jew, the boy's large, blank eyes, and Picasso's use of the color blue all help evoke a sense of the desperation and sadness of poverty, and the human condition as a whole.

From Barcelona to Paris

Between 1900 and 1904, Picasso traveled between Barcelona and Paris eight times. These two cities provided him with a variety of inspirational sources.

THE CAPITAL OF CATALONIA

Barcelona is the capital of Catalonia, a region of Spain with its own language and a very strong sense of culture independent from the rest of Spain. Here Picasso was introduced to pre-Roman Iberian sculpture and Roman art, but also to more modern influences. A style known as Catalan Gothic emerged in the late 19th century, led by the architect Antoni Gaudí (1852-1926).

◄ The Casa Batillo in Barcelona, designed by Antoni Gaudí.

▲ A pre-Roman Iberian bronze of a goddess made in Spain in the 7th century B.C.

Gaudí's work is often seen as a forerunner of Surrealism, a style that Picasso would experiment with himself later in his career (see page 24).

THE CAPITAL OF THE ART WORLD

Barcelona had a small, active art community, but it was tiny in comparison to Paris. The French capital had over 20 art "salons" which exhibited the work of over 1,000 artists. Wealthy collectors of modern art came to Paris from all over Europe and the United States to buy from these salons. It's no surprise that Paris acted like a magnet to young artists hoping to make a name for themselves.

TIMELINE ▶

1904	1905	Autumn 1905	January 1906	Spring 1906	October 1906
Picasso makes final move to Paris and takes a studio at the "Bateau-Lavoir." He meets Fernande Olivier. Blue Period ends.	Picasso's Pink Period begins. He paints circus themes and creates his first sculptures.	Picasso meets Gertrude and Leo Stein.	Vollard buys most of Pink Period paintings. Picasso is financially secure for the first time.	Picasso meets artists Matisse and Derain through the Steins.	Death of Cézanne. His influence shows in Picasso's work as Pink Period ends.

LIVING IN PARIS

In Paris, Picasso wandered around the museums and galleries, including the Louvre, where he could study art from many different periods and cultures. He sketched exotic art on display from ancient Egypt, Africa, and Japan. He also saw first-hand the work of Impressionist Edgar Degas (1834-1917) and Henri de Toulouse-Lautrec (1839-1906).

Picasso soaked up all of these different influences and ideas. Through his Blue Period and the Pink (or Rose) Period that followed, he featured the people who populated his Bohemian lifestyle (see panel), reflecting the social reality of the work of Degas and

▲ *Woman in the Café*, **Edgar Degas, 1877.** Degas liked to paint images of everyday life in Paris. Picasso was also attracted to this subject matter.

Toulouse-Lautrec. He also became interested in the work of Paul Cézanne (1839-1906) and Henri Matisse (1869-1954).

AMERICAN BUYERS

Picasso began to sell more of his work, particularly to the American collectors Gertrude and Leo Stein. In 1906, he painted Gertrude Stein's portrait, but just before he finished it, he whited out her face and replaced its naturalistic contours with something much flatter and mask-like. It was the beginning of a dramatic change in Picasso's art.

▲ In 1904, Picasso moved to a studio in an old piano factory in Montmartre (to the right of this picture). Max Jacob named the house the "Bateau-Lavoir," or wash boat, because of its shape and damp, creaky conditions.

THE BOHEMIAN LIFESTYLE

In each of his visits to Paris, and when he finally settled there in 1904, Picasso stayed in Montmartre. The area was popular with emerging artists because it was cheap. Picasso went to the cafés with other "Bohemian" artists and socialized with all classes of people, from poor intellectuals to street entertainers. He made many new friends, including the poet Max Jacob. At one time, the two shared a room: Picasso slept there during the day while Jacob was at work and, at night, Jacob slept while Picasso worked on his paintings. Picasso would often paint at night for the rest of his life.

A New Style of Art

INFLUENCES AT WORK

In *Les Demoiselles d'Avignon*, Picasso was clearly influenced by African and early Iberian sculpture (see page 14), although he was not likely to admit this. Another striking influence was the painter Cézanne, who once said, "Treat nature by the cylinder, the sphere, and the cone, everything in proper perspective, so that each side of the object or plane tends towards a central point."

In 1907 Picasso presented his latest work, *Les Demoiselles d'Avignon*, to his friends. They were horrified – he had taken the Classical subject of the female body and made it angular and ugly, not beautiful. Only one person seemed to like the painting, a young German collector called Daniel-Henry Kahnweiler. He and Picasso formed a professional and personal relationship that would last a lifetime.

▲ A Babuka tribe mask from central-east Africa. The woman's face in the top right of *Les Demoiselles d'Avignon* shows the same painted texturing.

▲ *Village of Gardanne*, Paul Cézanne, 1885-86. Cézanne often constructed his landscapes through simple blocks of color.

OVERCOMING SHOCK

As his friends and critics looked more closely at the painting, its importance became clear. Picasso was rebelling against traditional Western painting. He had used a combination of ideas from all over the world to create something completely different. One artist Georges Braque (1882-1963), who saw the picture and initially hated it, began to experiment with similar techniques. A new art genre, or style, had begun – Cubism.

When Picasso painted in the Cubist style, he emphasized the importance of form over everything else, including color. He depicted his subject in geometric terms – cylinders, cones, and cubes. What made the style more extraordinary was that Picasso painted an object from many different angles and used more than one light source. By doing this, it became possible to show a face or a body simultaneously, in profile and facing front.

TIMELINE ▶

Early 1907	July 1907	November 1907	1908	Summer 1909
Picasso begins work on *Les Demoiselles d'Avignon*. He sees African sculpture.	*Les Demoiselles* is completed. Picasso meets Kahnweiler who becomes his only dealer.	Braque comes to see *Les Demoiselles* in Picasso's studio.	Picasso paints numerous nudes, influenced by African sculpture. Braque shows Picasso his first Cubist pictures – they begin to work together.	Picasso visits Barcelona and Horta de San Juan and paints first Cubist landscapes, clearly influenced by Cézanne.

Les Demoiselles d'Avignon, 1907

oil on canvas, 90 x 92 in (243.9 x 233.7 cm), Museum of Modern Art, New York, New York

The form of the figures in this painting, their distorted and angular bodies, was very important to Picasso. Color is only used to separate the shapes of the bodies from the foreground and background.

"Look Pablo, this painting of yours, it's like making us eat tow [cloth fibers] and drink petrol to spit fire."

Georges Braque talking about Les Demoiselles d'Avignon

Experiments With Cubism

Picasso's reputation grew and, with it, his wealth. One painting, the *Family of Saltimbanques* was sold at auction for over 11,500 Francs (about $1,500), which was a huge sum at the time. He moved to Montparnasse, a more stylish part of Paris.

A CREATIVE PARTNERSHIP

Picasso worked with Braque, now a close friend. Braque described their relationship as being like "two mountain climbers roped together." Together, they pushed their experiments with Cubism further, taking their splintered images to a point where the subject often could not be recognized. They tried different techniques too, such as collage and reliefs.

The two artists' peace was shattered by the start of World War I in August of 1914. Braque went to fight for France against Germany. Picasso, being Spanish, did not have to fight. He continued working in Paris, moving to the suburbs in 1916.

◄ *Woman and Guitar*, Georges Braque, 1913. Picasso and Braque fed off each other's ideas. It was Braque who first suggested introducing words into their Cubist pictures.

► An illustration showing French troops charging German lines. World War I started in 1914 and lasted 4 years. Braque fought for France until 1915, when he was badly wounded.

COLLAGE

The Cubist artists used photographs, newspaper cuttings, and other objects to stick onto their canvases – a technique called collage. Sometimes the photos and cuttings were relevant to the picture's meaning and other times they were used just for their textural qualities. The cut out shapes of collage were perfect for the Cubist goal, which was to show objects in their most simplified form.

TIMELINE ▶

March 1911	July 1911	Autumn 1911	1912	1913	1914
Picasso has his first exhibition in New York.	Picasso and Braque go to Céret in the Pyrenees. They return there regularly over the next 3 years.	Picasso's relationship with Fernande ends. His new love is Eva Gouel.	Picasso develops Cubism still further, creating both 3-D reliefs and using collage. He has his first exhibition in London.	Picasso's father dies.	*Family of Saltimbanques* sells for 11,500F. Picasso paints "pointillist" pictures. World War I begins.

Bottle, Glass, and Violin, 1912

Charcoal and pastel paper, 18 $^1/_2$ x 24 $^2/_5$ (47 x 62 cm), Moderna Museet, Stockholm, Sweden

Picasso uses the simple cut-out shapes of collage to represent real objects – a bottle, glass, and violin. Black lines drawn with charcoal help define the objects.

"He reduces everything, figures, sites, and houses to simple geometric shapes, like cubes."

Art critic Louis Vauxcelles on Braque.
His remarks led to the use of the phrase "Cubism"

A Ballet and a Ballerina

DESIGNS FOR THE BALLET

Jean Cocteau was an avante-garde poet known for his enthusiasm for combining the arts. He had written the storyline for *Parade*, working closely with its composer Erik Satie and the director of the Ballets Russes, Sergei Diaghilev. Picasso designed the set and costumes. The experimental ballet provided Picasso with a perfect opportunity to combine his Cubist style with a vibrant, colorful realism. The effect, one viewer wrote, was "super real … a manifestation of the new spirit."

Programme des Ballets Russes

▲ The program for *Parade* on its first perfomance in Paris. The Chinese juggler print was based on a watercolor by Picasso.

In 1917 Picasso traveled to Rome, Italy, at the request of the French poet Jean Cocteau (1889-1963) to work on the stage design for the Ballets Russes' latest performance, *Parade*.

◀ Olga Kokhlova with Picasso in Paris, 1917. Olga was born in St. Petersburg, Russia in 1881. She was the daughter of a Russian general.

There he met Olga Kokhlova, a dancer with the ballet company. Picasso fell in love. He followed her and the ballet company to Barcelona, where Picasso was welcomed by his old friends. It was here that he painted *Portrait of Olga in an Armchair* in a style so different from Cubism that his critics could no longer categorize him as the enemy of Classical beauty.

CREATING PERFECTION

Working from photographs he had taken of Olga, Picasso tried to capture a perfect likeness in her portrait. He deliberately left the background of the painting unfinished to focus attention on Olga. Picasso poured all of his feelings into this painting, revealing the importance of his new found love.

When the ballet company left Barcelona for South America, Olga traveled back to Paris with Picasso. They were married there in 1918.

TIMELINE ▶

1915	1916	1917	1918	1919
Eva dies after a long illness. Picasso meets Jean Cocteau.	Picasso asked to design stage set for new production. *Les Demoiselles d'Avignon* shown in public for the first time.	Picasso travels to Rome to work on Ballets Russes set. He meets Olga Kokhlova. He follows the ballet group to Barcelona.	Back in Paris, Picasso marries Olga. Picasso is working in a variety of art styles and has a new dealer, Paul Rosenberg.	Picasso meets young Spanish artist Joan Miró. He works in London on a new ballet for three months.

Portrait of Olga in an Armchair, 1917
oil on canvas, 51 x 34 2/3 in (130 x 88 cm), Musée Picasso, Paris, France

Olga's face has a serious and dreamlike expression almost like a mannequin's. Her relaxed pose and flowing clothes emphasize her simple beauty.

The Family Man

▲ Picasso in his studio in 1929. Several different styles of art can be seen in the clutter around him, as well as a metal sculpture on the table.

Picasso's life was changing again. He and his new wife moved to an even-more fashionable part of Paris and began to entertain and be entertained by Paris's high society.

In February of 1921, Olga gave birth to their only child, Paulo. Picasso adored his son and spent hours watching him play. He once decorated one of Paulo's toy cars, painting its floor with a checked carpet. Paulo was furious – a real car wouldn't have a checked floor.

▲ Paulo Picasso, around age two. Picasso featured Paulo in many of his paintings in the 1920s, including one based on this photograph.

USING DIFFERENT STYLES

After 1918 and during the 1920s, Picasso did not limit himself to painting in any one style. Friends criticized this versatility, saying that he was abandoning Cubism. After World War I, the Cubist style had become unpopular in France, as it was seen as a German art form. However, Picasso still created Cubist art alongside his other work. He explained that he painted using a style that best suited his subject, rather than always painting in one style.

EXAGGERATED PROPORTIONS

The changes in Picasso's life also affected his art. He often painted a mother and child during this time – a theme he returned to throughout his life. He also experimented with a variety of art styles. In particular, he began to paint monumental figures, exaggerating their proportions to simplify their form. This style, which is often described as neoclassical, made the figures he painted immensely powerful but somehow not of this world.

TIMELINE ▶

1920	1921	1923	1925	1927
Picasso works on sets for the ballet *Pulcinella*. He spends time with Olga on the fashionable Riviera coast of southern France.	Birth of Paulo. Picasso paints theme of mother and child again and again. His neoclassical style emerging.	Cubism is attacked as a spent force. André Breton, soon to found Surrealism, defends Picasso.	First signs of tension in Picasso's marriage. He contributes to first Surrealist exhibition in Paris.	Picasso meets 17-year-old Marie-Thérèse Walter, who becomes his mistress.

Mother and Child, 1921

oil on canvas, 56 ¹/4 x 68 in (142.9 x 172.7 cm), The Art Institute of Chicago, Illinois

Picasso chose to paint this image in his neoclassical style, using the Classical figures that he studied in his education (see page 9), but exaggerating their scale to give them an almost god-like feel. However, in this painting, the delicate colors and the soft rounded forms give the painting a sense of gentleness and affection.

"Each time I have had something to say, I said it in the manner in which I felt it ought to be said."

Pablo Picasso

Creating Monsters

CHÂTEAU DE BOISGELOUP

Picasso loved to travel. Everywhere he went he created a chaotic studio, claiming he found his inspiration in disorder. In 1930, Picasso bought a beautiful 17th-century château outside Paris in the village of Boisgeloup. Picasso used its former stables as a studio, working on sculpture in particular. He had become friends with the sculptor Julio González (1876-1942), who encouraged Picasso to develop this side of his art.

Picasso also used the château as an escape from his arguments with Olga. Sometimes he was accompanied by Marie-Thérèse Walter, a young woman with whom he was having an affair. She bore him a daughter, Maïa, in 1935.

▲ In his art, Picasso drew on images of the bull and bullfights which had fascinated him since childhood. Their influence became particularly strong during his "monster" period.

The cultured and privileged world that Olga created for Picasso soon began to stifle him and they frequently argued. He told friends that he wanted to "liberate the green lawn from its respectability." The couple eventually separated in 1935. As the marriage deteriorated, Picasso was also being drawn into a new artistic movement called "Surrealism." This combination of events caused Picasso to explode into a new and aggressive style – often described as his "monster" period.

SURREALIST INFLUENCES

The Surrealist movement had begun in the early 1920s. The Surrealists believed that art should express the unconscious mind, exploring the world of dreams and hidden memories. Its founders acknowledged that Picasso's art and Cubism had already influenced their ideas. Now Picasso was influenced by them, attracted by their belief that the everyday objects and ordinary scenes which fascinated him could have a deeper, unconscious significance.

▲ The Château Boisgeloup to the north of Paris was a retreat for Picasso. He went there to concentrate on his work.

TIMELINE ▶

1928	1930	1932	1934	1935
Picasso meets the sculptor Gonzalez and works on sculpture for the first time since 1914.	Picasso buys Château Boisgeloup, north of Paris. There is a "monstrous" aspect to much of his work.	Major Picasso retrospective (236 works) in Paris and Zürich. The first Picasso catalog published.	Picasso travels to Spain with Olga and Paulo to see bullfights. He paints many bullfighting pictures, using several different styles.	Picasso separates from Olga. Marie-Thérèse gives birth to their daughter, Maïa.

Figures by the Sea, 1931

oil on canvas, 51 3/8 x 77 in (130.5 x 195.5 cm), Musée Picasso, Paris, France

During his "monster" period, Picasso painted many images where the human form became something distorted and violent. The figures in this painting appear to be kissing, which is normally an act of affection, yet here it seems cruel and aggressive. The seaside setting is strangely enclosed, giving a dreamlike sense of claustrophobia. Picasso's work was often affected by his private life, and images such as this one may reflect the poor state of his relationship with Olga at the time.

"We claim him as one of ours, even though it is impossible... Surrealism has but to pass where Picasso has already passed, and where he will pass in the future."

André Breton, founder of the Surrealists, talking about Picasso

Bombs Dropped on Guernica

On April 26, 1937, German warplanes bombed the Basque town of Guernica killing 1,664 people and injuring almost 900. Homes were left in flames and the market square was completely destroyed.

Guernica, 1937

oil on canvas, 137 $^1/_2$ x 305 $^3/_4$ in (349.3 x 776.6 cm), Museo National Central de Arte Reina Sofía, Madrid, Spain

Guernica was bombed as part of the ongoing Spanish Civil War. Picasso was horrified at the savage attack and conjured up all of his feelings to paint *Guernica*. Picasso made 45 sketches and studies before he started on the main painting. To give it a historical feeling, he only used shades of black and white as in a photograph. He used imagery from the bullring to represent the unfolding story – the bull represents evil and the horse, standing among the broken bodies, the bravery of the people of Guernica. The dramatic result conveyed a horror of war in any age.

THE WEEPING WOMAN

Guernica was first shown to the public in July of 1937, but Picasso was still obsessed with the subject, returning to it and its imagery again and again over the coming months. He painted *Weeping Woman*, one of his final explorations of the subject, at the end of the year. The human tragedy is represented by the grief of one woman, Dora Maar. She was a photographer who had become close friends with Picasso. He painted her in the Cubist style, using bright colors to reflect her outgoing personality. He contrasted these colors with the violent white area created by her tears, suggesting the death and destruction at Guernica.

TIMELINE ▶

1936	1937	January 1939	September 1939
The Spanish Civil War begins. Picasso meets Yugoslav photographer Dora Maar.	After German air attack on Guernica, Picasso paints gigantic mural for the Spanish pavilion. *Guernica* is the culmination of his "monster period."	Death of Picasso's mother. Franco wins Spanish Civil War shortly after. Later that month, Picasso paints Marie-Thérèse and Dora Maar in same pose on same day.	Germany, under Adolf Hitler's command, invades Poland and World War II begins.

Weeping Woman, 1937
oil on canvas, 23 $^2/_3$ x 19 $^1/_4$ in (60 x 49 cm), Tate Modern, London, England

Living Through War

The Spanish Civil War began in 1936. It was fought between the Spanish Republican government, which had been elected to power in 1931, and the Fascist forces under the control of General Franco. Fascism was a growing political movement in the 1930s. Its right-wing ideas included a strong central government and extreme national pride. Franco gained outside support from Germany and Italy, who both had Fascist governments, enabling him to win power in Spain in 1939.

A USEFUL EXPERIMENT

The German government that supported Franco was controlled by the Nazi party, lead by Adolf Hitler. He saw the Spanish Civil War as a chance to try out the new ideas on warfare the Germans had developed, including blanket bombing. The terrible effectiveness of the attack on Guernica and others gave Hitler the confidence to push for Germany to

▲ The aftermath of the bombing of Guernica, 1937. We have become accustomed to images of destruction on this scale, but in 1937 it was truly shocking.

have increasing power in Europe. Eventually he went too far, and, as the Spanish Civil War ended, a new conflict began – World War II (1939-45).

WARTIME PARIS

Picasso's day-to-day life in France had remained unchanged by the Spanish Civil War, but this was not the case for World War II. In 1940, Paris was attacked by the German army and taken over. Picasso was trapped in the city. He continued to work, but supplies and restrictions hampered him. Unlike some other artists, Picasso was not seduced by offers from the Nazis. He continued to paint revolutionary paintings under their noses.

◄ The swastika flag, symbol of Nazi Germany, flies over Paris in 1940.

▲ U.S. troops march through the Arc de Triomphe in August of 1944 during the liberation of Paris from the Nazis.

that he was saved from this by the intervention of one of Hitler's favorite sculptors, Arno Breker. Breker made sure that Picasso had materials to create sculptures, even when the Germans were melting metal statues down to help with the war effort.

IN THE MIDST OF BATTLE
Picasso's paintings during the war reflected what he saw and felt. The subject matter usually depicted the war – animal skulls lit only by candles and sharp, twisted knives. In 1944, the liberation of Paris was fought around Picasso's studio. Amidst the gunfire and explosions, Picasso painted, singing at the top of his voice to drown out the noise from the streets.

A DEGENERATE ARTIST
The Nazis labeled Picasso a "degenerate Bolshevik," meaning that he was, according to them, an immoral rebel. It was obvious that he hated the Nazis because of his painting of Guernica. One day, when the Gestapo, the Nazis' secret police, came to search his studio, an officer saw a photograph of *Guernica*. He asked Picasso, "Did you do this?" "No," said the painter, "you did."

As a result of the Nazis' attitude, it was hard for Picasso to keep his career going. He was able to meet with friends, such as Ambroise Vollard and Jaime Sabartés everyday in a café; however, he only held one minor show. The Nazis put him on a register for possible transportation to Germany for slave labor, but it seems

◀ Picasso in his studio in Paris shortly after the liberation of Paris, 1944. A tomato plant stands on the windowsill, with a painting of it by Picasso propped up underneath.

Emerging From a Nightmare

▲ *Bull I*, 11 1/3 x 16 1/4 in (28.9 x 41 cm), **lithograph, 1945.** This is the first in a series of eleven progressive images Picasso made working on the same lithograph. Initially realistic, Picasso changed the lithograph to focus on the bull's shape.

LITHOGRAPHY

In 1945, Braque introduced Picasso to Fernand Mourlot, a lithographer. Lithography is a form of printing using an image etched on stone. Picasso liked the technique because he could print from the lithograph at different stages of working on it, showing how an image evolved.

Together Picasso and Mourlot produced many lithographs – over 200 in three years. These included portraits of Françoise, and pictures of bulls and mythological creatures, such as centaurs (half man, half horse).

During the war years, people had heard little news of Picasso and his work. When Paris was liberated in 1944, Picasso was overwhelmed with visitors, especially American and British people. This was a sign of the international fame Picasso had by this time. He was also a controversial figure. At a Paris exhibition he had in 1944, there were violent protests from both art students and right-wing conservatives.

The end of the war seemed like the end of a nightmare – Picasso had seen a lot of suffering and lost many friends, both in the war and in concentration camps. Now his life seemed renewed. His paintings still reflected the war but also had a new sense of order. He began to experiment again, this time with techniques in printing.

A NEW LOVE

During the war, Picasso had met Françoise Gilot, who was also a painter. Their relationship became even closer after the war, and this new love contributed to Picasso's sense of well-being. The pair spent a lot of time in the south of France near the sea, which Picasso called "his landscape," where he was happy.

◀ **Picasso first met Françoise Gilot in Paris, in May of 1943. The sophisticated daughter of a French industrialist, she abandoned her study of philosophy to take up painting.**

TIMELINE ▶

1940	1941	1943	1944	1945	1946
Paris falls to Germany. Picasso still able to go to Boisgeloup.	Picasso writes a Surrealist play called *Desire Caught by the Tail*. He is no longer allowed to leave Paris.	Picasso meets painter Françoise Gilot.	Max Jacob dies in a concentration camp. Paris is liberated. Picasso joins the Communist Party.	End of World War II. Picasso begins working with lithography.	Picasso takes Françoise to Nice to see Matisse. He makes paintings and lithographs of her.

Still Life With Pitcher, Candle, and Enamel Pot, 1945

oil on canvas, 32 $^1/4$ x 41 $^3/4$ in (82 x 106 cm), Musée National d'Art Moderne, Paris, France

In this still life, everything is in its own space. The objects chosen reflect the hardship of the war years, but they have clear form and shape, and new color is introduced on the pot and candlestick – vibrant blue and yellow. Light and shade are defined with thick black lines. Picasso has given everyday objects dignity and definition.

"Since line and color are my weapons, I have used them to try to gain a continually greater understanding of the world of mankind, so that this understanding might give us all a continually greater freedom."

Pablo Picasso

Playing With Children

▲ Pottery for sale on the streets of Vallauris. Picasso's fame helped revive the town's ceramics industry.

WORKING IN VALLAURIS

Picasso's work at Vallauris was full of fun and playfulness. The ceramic jugs, vases, and figures that Picasso made there were inspired by doves, owls, bulls, and women's heads. He produced several thousand pieces in just a few years (you can see him at work on page 35). However, Picasso created many sculptures at this time, such as his *Baboon With Young* (right). In this sculpture, he used plaster to combine objects that he found lying around – a toy car for the baboon's head and jug handles for its ears – then cast the whole thing in bronze. The choice of materials reflected the playful and childlike subject of the monkey.

Picasso and Françoise Gilot had two children together, Claude, born in 1947, and Paloma in 1949. Picasso lived with his family in Provence in the south of France, buying a villa in the hills above Vallauris. The pretty village was full of ceramicists and potters, and Picasso was attracted by their craft. From the summer of 1947, he had begun to explore pottery further, experimenting with shape and skills that the potters themselves had never tried.

"Still making babies at my age, how ridiculous!"

Pablo Picasso age 66

▶ Picasso in 1949, swimming with Claude in the Mediterranean.

A YOUTHFUL OLD AGE

Picasso loved being in Vallauris and spent a lot of time with his young family. He taught them to paint and swim. He loved their cheerfulness and liveliness. It was difficult to remember that Picasso was growing old – he celebrated his seventieth birthday in 1951.

Public interest in Picasso continued. People heard that he and his family were regularly on the beaches of Provence. Tourists and photographers came to catch a glimpse of the famous artist, something Picasso did not always like.

TIMELINE ▶

1947	1948	1949	1950	1951
Françoise gives birth to Claude. Picasso creates his first ceramics at Vallauris.	Picasso moves to La Galloise, a villa in Vallauris.	Picasso draws *The Dove*, a symbol of peace used by the World Peace Congress. Françoise gives birth to Paloma (which is Spanish for dove).	Picasso exhibits at the Venice Biennale. He is awarded the Lenin Peace Prize and named honorary citizen of Vallauris.	Picasso continues working on ceramics at Vallauris. There is a retrospective exhibition of his work in Tokyo, Japan.

Baboon With Young, 1951

bronze (after original plaster with metal, ceramic elements, and two toy cars), 21 3/4 x 13 1/4 x 20 3/4 in (55.3 x 33.7 x 52.7 cm), Private Collection

By casting his sculpture in bronze, Picasso shows the dignity and strength of the bond between mother and child even though they are monkeys.

A Man of Many Talents

One of the ways Picasso revealed his genius was partly in the variety of his work. He was never tied to any one technique or medium, instead he went out of his way to explore different ways to depict the same and different subjects. This was his inspiration – he knew how to draw and visualize, but what could he do with this ability?

THE DRAFTSMAN

He produced line drawings using pencils, charcoal, as well as lithographs (see page 30) and etchings. Picasso had learned how to produce an etching in Spain, and he continued to use this method throughout his career. Etchings are made when a design is cut into a metal plate using acid. Once created, the plate can be used to print the image again and again. Much later in life, around 1959, he discovered the technique of linocuts – artists cut into linoleum to create a printable picture.

THE PAINTER

In his paintings, Picasso used watercolors, especially during his Blue and Pink

▲ Picasso at work on a sculpture, c. 1950. Beside him stands the figure of *Girl Jumping a Rope* which was assembled from wicker baskets and cake pans. He would later cast it in bronze.

Periods, as well as oil on canvas. During the war, when materials were in short supply, Picasso would paint on whatever surface he could get hold of, such as wooden planks. He also mixed paint with other materials, such as paper and wood veneers when he worked on collages (see page 19).

THE SCULPTOR

Picasso's work was not limited by two-dimensional representation. He produced hundreds of sculptures, sometimes just working in metal wire and wood, other times in bronze. He began to incorporate objects that he found around him, such as wicker baskets, palm leaves, cake pans, and baby strollers. Some of these works would then be cast in bronze (see page 33). Others he simply left as they were. The idea of using "found objects" (or *objets trouvés*) was not a new one, but Picasso managed to create strikingly imaginative images that made the viewer look at everyday things in a new way – something he had been concerned with ever since developing Cubism.

▼ *Bull's Head*, 1942, bicycle saddle and handlebars, 13 1/6 x 17 1/8 x 7 1/2 in (33.5 x 43.5 x 19 cm), Musée Picasso, Paris, France. By creating a bull's head with parts of a bicycle, Picasso makes us look at the bicycle parts in a new way but at the same time manages to convey the great sense of power and strength of the bull.

▼ Picasso working on his pottery at Vallauris. The pot he is working on includes both a female face on the central section and an owl's face on the upper one.

THE POTTER

Picasso produced most of his ceramics during his time at Vallauris (see page 32). This was his playground, a way of experimenting and just having fun. He began by decorating ready-made ceramic shapes with colored slips (colored liquid clays) and glazes, but ended up working with the clay himself and stretching the boundaries of what potters could traditionally do.

THE PHOTOGRAPHER

Picasso was not even limited to physical materials. Using photography, he was able to create images from light. He would rapidly draw a line image with a torch in front of a camera. At the same time, he took a picture using a long exposure – so the light image he created was captured on film.

Inspiration From the Past

Picasso wanted to find somewhere to escape from the glare of publicity that surrounded him. Continuous press attention contributed to the breakdown of his relationship with Françoise, and in 1953, she and their children moved to Paris. In Perpignan earlier that year, Picasso had met Jacqueline Roque. She became his new love and, in 1955, they moved to La Californie, a secluded villa in the hills above Cannes on the Mediterranean.

VARIATIONS ON A THEME

As his life settled down again, Picasso continued his experimentation. He began work on paintings that took their inspiration from art of the past. Manet's *Luncheon on the Grass* (below), painted in 1863, inspired one such series.

▲ **Picasso (left) with his old friend Jaime Sabartés at La Californie, 1956, holding ceramic masks made by Picasso. Picasso entertained many old friends at La Californie.**

▲ *Luncheon on the Grass*, **Edouard Manet, 1863.** Manet's painting caused a scandal when it was first shown because of the naked women outside in the company of clothed men.

OLD MASTERS, NEW LIFE

Edouard Manet (1832-83) was not the only painter that inspired Picasso. He also reinterpreted the Spanish master Diego Velázquez (1599-1660), producing a series of works based on *Las Meninas* (see page 8), and the French painter Eugène Delacroix (1798-1863). When working on these variations, Picasso made hundreds of studies. He explained his way of working by saying, "The fact that I paint such a large number of studies is simply part of my manner of working. I do a hundred studies in a few days, whereas another painter might spend a hundred days on a single painting."

TIMELINE ▶

1953	1954	1955	1957	1958	1961
Picasso meets Jacqueline Roque in Perpignan. He and Françoise separate.	Death of Matisse. Picasso begins work as a tribute to him.	Buys La Californie, a villa in Cannes, southern France.	Picasso works at La Californie on variations of Velázquez's *Las Meninas*.	Picasso buys Château Vauvenargues near Aix-en-Provence mainly to house his huge art collection.	Picasso marries Jacqueline at Vallauris. He celebrates his 80th birthday.

Luncheon on Grass – After Manet, 1960
oil on canvas, 50 $^3/_4$ x 76 $^3/_4$ in (129 x 195 cm), Musée Picasso, Paris, France

This is one of 27 pictures Picasso painted based on Manet's picture, each one is slightly different. Comparing Picasso's work with Manet's, it is clear that the form and style of Picasso's picture is entirely his own. He did not simply copy the work of other painters. It is as though he is comparing himself to the masters of the past, taking on their work and elaborating their themes and skills to produce something new. At the same time, this method encourages us to look at the original painting with a fresh eye.

"If there is something to steal, I steal it!"

Pablo Picasso

"Painting Is Stronger Than Me"

▲ Picasso in his studio shortly before his ninetieth birthday, surrounded by his work in progress. In his later years, Picasso concentrated mainly on drawing and prints, but he continued to work on larger pieces.

UNFINISHED ART

"Finish a work! Complete a picture? How absurd," Picasso once said to a friend. "To finish an object means to finish it, to destroy it, to rob it of its soul, to give to it the 'puntilla' [death blow] as to the bull in the ring." Picasso saw his paintings as living pieces, with no end and no final definition. He said his art was always an exploration: "One never stops seeking because one never finds." To the viewer, this also has to be true. You can never pin down Picasso's work and describe it within set boundaries. This is what makes him so exceptional and so fascinating.

In 1961, Picasso and Jacqueline married. He was nearly 80. The couple moved to a new villa above Cannes, Notre-Dame-de-Vie, but they also spent time at the beautiful Chateau de Vauvenargues, which Picasso had bought in 1959 to house his ever-growing collection of art.

Picasso continued to produce art as though he was a thirty year old. He described his need to paint: "Painting is stronger than me, she makes me do her will." In 1970, there was a huge exhibition of his most recent work at Avignon, not far from his home. People were amazed at the energy of the work produced – he seemed immortal! However, on April 8, 1973, Picasso died. He was 91 and had never stopped working.

▲ The magnificent Vauvenargues, a 14th-century château near Aix-en-Provence.

THE EYES OF AN ARTIST

In his last years, Picasso worked on many self-portraits and a dominant feature of all these images is his eyes. They assume an intensity and proportion that illustrate the artist's sense of their importance. It is almost as though he was determined to leave behind images of himself still looking intently at the world around him. As his friend, Matisse once said, "Picasso sees everything."

TIMELINE ▶

1963	1964	1965	1967	1968	1971	April 8,1973
Museo Picasso opens in Barcelona. Death of Braque and Cocteau.	Françoise Gilot publishes *Life with Picasso*, against Picasso's wishes.	Picasso works on theme of "painter and model." His last trip to Paris.	Picasso refuses French Legion of Honor award.	Death of Sabartés. Picasso gives 58 pictures from *Las Meninas* series to the Museo Picasso.	Picasso celebrates his 90th birthday.	Picasso dies at Mougins. He is later buried in the grounds of Château Vauvenargues.

Self-Portrait, 1972

pastel on paper, 25 7/8 x 19 7/8 in (65.7 x 50.5 cm), Fuji Television Gallery, Tokyo, Japan

Picasso drew this self-portrait the year before he died. He shows very simply the deeply lined face of old age. The features, particularly the eyes and nose, now dominate and seem huge compared to the face's sunken cheeks and the shrunken shoulders beneath it.

Picasso's Legacy

◀ People walk through the Musée Picasso, Paris. However, Picasso's work can be seen throughout the world. No modern art museum is complete without it.

Picasso's death was a shock to the world – people thought that he was still so full of life and vitality. He was still creating work that provoked and expressed emotion. It is estimated that in his long life, Picasso created over 20,000 works of art and these paintings, etchings, sculptures, and ceramics stand as a testimony to his artistic genius.

THE GIFT OF ART

Before he died, Picasso left many paintings to places that meant a great deal to him during his life. In 1963, the Museo Picasso had opened in Barcelona. Its initial collection was donated by Picasso's friend Jaime Sabartés, but, after his friend died in 1968, Picasso continued to give works to the Museo. Today the collection is housed in a beautiful medieval palace.

In an agreement with the French government, Picasso left a personal selection of his work to France – enough to fill a museum. In 1985 the Musée Picasso opened in Paris. This museum contains 203 paintings, 191 sculptures, 85 ceramics, and over 3,000 drawings, engravings, and manuscripts that span his life as an artist.

"A work of art must make a man react, feel strongly, start creating too, if only in his imagination. He must be seized by the throat and shaken up; he has to be made aware of the world he's living in and for that he must first be jolted out of it."

Pablo Picasso

> *"You expect me to tell you: what is art? If I knew, I would keep my knowledge to myself."*
>
> *Pablo Picasso*

▲ *Reclining Figure*, **Henry Moore, 1936.** The monumental figures of Henry Moore are reminiscent of Picasso during his "monster" period (see page 24). Both men were influenced by the Surrealists.

THE FATHER OF MODERN ART

It has been said that Picasso was the father of modern art, with his diversity of style and desire to challenge the way objects were visually represented. The 20th century became filled with movements that Picasso created, flirted with, influenced, or inspired. In Cubism, Picasso explored the nature of shape and these themes were developed further by artists such as Henry Moore (1898-1986), Francis Bacon (1909-92), and Jacob Epstein (1880-1959).

However, Picasso's sheer diversity opens his influence to virtually every artist working today, even if it is not consciously acknowledged. David Hockney (b. 1937) has explored the ideas of multiple perspectives in his paintings, while Sir Eduardo Paolozzi (b. 1924) has experimented with geometric forms in both sculpture and painting. The young artists of today, who create art in every conceiveable media and with a vast range of materials, do so in part because Picasso showed them the way.

◄ Chris Ofili, winner of the 1998 Turner Prize, stands in front of his work, *Through the Grapevine*. Like Picasso, Ofili is known for his experimentation with materials – including elephant dung – and his use of *objets trouvés*.

41

Picasso Versus Matisse

Picasso and Henri Matisse were creating art at the same time during the first half of the twentieth century. The art collector Gertrude Stein introduced the two men in Paris in 1906. They immediately recognized each other's great talent, and were encouraged to be rivals by Stein. This competition proved inspiring.

Matisse wanted to express an affirmative vision of the world… Picasso dared to question everything. Matisse was generous… Picasso had a flair for the new, the unexpected. Matisse intensified the interplay of color, while Picasso's revolt was aimed at structure and form. Their polarity was mutually invigorating… they needed each other as a permanent challenge.

◀ Françoise Gilot, mother of two of Picasso's children, described Matisse and Picasso's relationship in her book *Life with Picasso*. The two artists clearly enjoyed their differences.

The personality of the artist asserts itself through the struggles it has to go through when pitted against other personalities. If the fight is fatal, it is a matter of destiny.

◀ Matisse recognized the benefits of a competitve relationship. In Picasso, he could be sure that the clash of personalities was evenly balanced but there was drama in the fight.

I must break away from tradition, break away from beauty, from sentimentality. This is my drama.

▲ Picasso also saw making art as a struggle – in his case, one fought between himself and established ideas on art.

TIMELINE ▶

1881	1895	1898	1902	1906	1911
October 25 Pablo Ruiz Picasso is born in Málaga, Spain. First son of José Ruiz Blasco and Maria Picasso y Lopez.	**1895** Father takes teaching post at La Lonja, the School of Fine Arts, Barcelona. Picasso studies there. Visits the Prado, Madrid.	**1898** Spends time in the village of Horta de San Juan.	**1902-03** Moves between Barcelona and Paris.	**1906** Paintings selling. Has financial security. Meets Matisse. Death of Cézanne. Pink Period ends.	**1911** First of 3 trips with Braque to the Pyrenees. Relationship with Fernande ends. New love is Eva Gouel.
1889 Completes his first painting, a bullfight.	**1896** Exhibits his first large-scale work, *The First Communion*.	**1900** His first solo exhibition held at *Els Quatre Gats*, Barcelona. Travels with Casagemas to Paris.	**1904** Makes final move to Paris. Meets Fernande Olivier. Blue Period ends.	**1907** Produces *Les Demoiselles d'Avignon*. Birth of Cubism. Meets Kahnweiler and Braque.	**1912** Develops Cubism still further. First London exhibition.
1891 The family move to La Coruña. Younger sister Conchita dies.	**1897** Starts at the Royal Academy, Madrid but leaves within months.	**February 1901** Casagemas's suicide.	**1905** Pink Period begins. Creates his first sculptures.	**1908** Begins to work with Braque.	**1913** Father dies.
		May 1901 Blue Period begins. Exhibition at Vollard's gallery.	**Autumn 1905** Meets Gertrude and Leo Stein.	**1911** First exhibition in New York.	**1914-18** World War I. **1915** Eva dies. Meets Jean Cocteau.

A LONG-TERM FRIENDSHIP

The admiration the two men felt for each other grew into a lifelong friendship. Picasso once tried to help Matisse over a creative block by painting a series of pictures which imitated Matisse's style. It worked – Matisse rose to the challenge by painting the pictures as he felt they should have been painted.

Basically, everything comes from the self. It's like having a sun with a thousand rays in your belly. The rest is nothing. It is solely for that, for example, that Matisse is Matisse. It is because he has sun in his belly.

▲ Picasso graphically described the creative fire which made Matisse a great artist. Matisse equally admired Picasso for his unique vision (see page 38).

We must talk to each other as much as we can. When one of us dies, there will be some things the other will never be able to talk of with anyone else.

◀ Later in life, Matisse and Picasso visited each other regularly and continued their conversations about their different approaches to art. Matisse wrote this letter to Picasso encouraging him to visit him again.

All things considered, there's only Matisse.

▲ Picasso was deeply saddened by Matisse's death in 1954. He often made this remark about his friend.

HENRI MATISSE

French artist, Henri Matisse was, alongside Picasso, the foremost painter of his time. He was admired for the beauty of his art, with its sensual line and luminous color. Born in Brittany in 1869, he left a career in law, in order to become an artist. He went to Paris where his use of color made him a natural member of the Fauves (the Wild Beasts), but thereafter was never strongly linked with any particular art movement. After 1916, he spent much of his time in the south of France. Before his death in 1954, too ill to paint, he continued to work by creating abstract art from cut-out paper shapes.

1917	1927	1935	1943	1953	1963
1917 Works on Ballets Russes set in Rome. Meets Olga Kokhlova.	**1927** Meets Marie-Thérèse Walter, who becomes his mistress.	**1935** Separates from Olga. Marie-Thérèse gives birth to Maïa.	**1943** Meets painter Françoise Gilot.	**1953** Meets Jacqueline Roque. Separates from Françoise.	**1963** Museo Picasso opens in Barcelona. Death of Braque and Cocteau.
1918 Marries Olga. Working in a variety of art styles.	**1928** Works with sculptor Gonzalez.	**1936** The Spanish Civil War begins.	**1944** Paris is liberated. Joins the Communist Party.	**1954** Death of Matisse.	**1967** Refuses French Legion of Honor.
1921 Birth of Paulo. Neoclassical style emerging.	**1930** Buys Château Boisgeloup, north of Paris. "Monstrous" aspect to his work.	**1937** Paints *Guernica*.	**1945** World War II ends. Works with lithography	**1957** Begins work on past master variations.	**1971** Celebrates his 90th birthday
1925 First signs of tension in marriage. He contributes to first Surrealist exhibition.	**1932** Major retrospective in Paris and Zürich. First Picasso catalog.	**1939** Mother dies. Franco wins Spanish Civil War. World War II begins.	**1947** Birth of Claude. Working on ceramics at Vallauris.	**1958** Buys Château Vauvenargues near Aix-en-Provence.	**April 8,1973** Dies at Mougins. Buried in grounds of Château Vauvenargues.
		1940 Living in Paris when Germany invades.	**1949** Birth of Paloma.	**1961** Marries Jacqueline. Celebrates his 80th birthday.	

Glossary

Art Nouveau: a decorative style which began about 1890, rejecting Classical lines. It was mainly used for ornaments.

avant-garde: describes new, experimental, or radical ideas. From the French for vanguard, the first troops into battle.

Bohemian: describes a person, often an artist or intellectual, who lives in a way that does not follow social conventions.

Bolshevik: a member of the Russian Communist Party, often used for Communists generally.

ceramics: artworks created by baking clay.

Classical: describes something from the period of European history which was dominated by the ancient Greek and then Roman civilizations.

collage: a picture made by pasting photographs, newspaper cuttings, string, labels, and other objects on to a flat surface.

Communist: a supporter of the political system first suggested by Karl Marx (1818-83) under which every one shares a country's goods and property.

concentration camp: a prison camp where civilians are held.

Cubism: the name of an art movement evolving in Paris around 1907 led by Picasso and Braque. The Cubists painted multiple angles of a person or object so they were all seen at once.

degenerate: something that has descended to a low moral, mental, or artistic level.

etching: a print on paper made from an engraved metal plate.

Fascism: an extreme right-wing political system where the government holds total power, and is usually focused around a charismatic leader.

Fauves: French for "wild beasts," the name given by a shocked critic in 1905 to a group of painters, including Henri Matisse and André Derain, who used bright, unnatural colors in their art.

glazes: the glass-based material used in ceramics to make an object waterproof and shiny.

Iberian: of Iberia, the peninsula occupied by Spain and Portugal.

Impressionist: A group based in Paris during the late nineteenth century who painted "impressions" of the world with broad brushstrokes of pure, unmixed color. The group included Claude Monet and Edgar Degas.·

linocut: a print on paper made from an image cut out of linoleum, a cloth-based material used to cover floors.

lithograph: a print on paper made from an engraved stone.

medium: (plural media), the means or method by which a person (in this case an artist) chooses to communicate.

Nazi: anything to do with the National Socialist German Workers Party, the extreme right-wing political party lead by Adolf Hitler that ruled Germany between 1933 and 1945.

neoclassical: describes a style which seeks to revive or develop Classical ideas of art.

objets trouvés: French for "found objects," the term used to describe everyday objects used to create art.

Old Masters: the name used to describe the greatest European painters from 1500-1800.

pointillist: paintings composed by using dots, or points, of color.

relief: a 3-dimensional image projected off a flat surface.

Renaissance: meaning rebirth, the European intellectual and artistic movement which began in 14th century Italy and was at its height in the 16th century, where Classical ideas were rediscovered or "reborn."

republican: describes a government where power is held by a person or persons elected by the people, not by a monarch.

Surrealism: an intellectual movement that began in the 1920s that tried to show the life of our unconscious minds and dreams. Its most famous artist is Salvador Dali, but it included writers and filmmakers.

slip: liquid clay, often colored.

Museums and Galleries

Picasso was working for over 70 years and in this time produced thousands of paintings, sculptures, etchings, lithographs, and ceramics. His work is exhibited all over the world, in both dedicated Picasso museums and in general museums of modern art. Some of these are listed below.

Even if you can't visit these galleries yourself, you may be able to visit their web sites. Gallery web sites often show pictures of the artworks they have on display. Some web sites even have virtual tours so that you can wander around while sitting in front of your computer at home or school! Most of the international web sites below have an option to view in English.

FRANCE
Musée Picasso
Hôtel Salé, 5, rue de Thorigny
75003 Paris

Picasso Museum
Chateau Grimaldi
06600 Antibes
www.antibes-juanlespins.com/eng/
art_culture/museums/picasso.html

**Centre national d'art et de culture
Georges Pompidou**
75191 Paris cedex 04
www.cnac-gp.fr/Pompidou/Home.nsf/docs/fhome

GERMANY
Graphikmuseum Pablo Picasso Münster
Königstrasse 5
48143 Münster
www.graphikmuseum.de

SPAIN
Centre Picasso de Horta
Antic Hospital
43596 Horta de Sant Joan
Catalunya
www.centrepicasso.org

Fundacíon Picasso
Plaza de la Merced 15
29012 Málaga
www.fundacionpicasso.es/en/index.html

Museo Nacional Centro de Arte Reina Sofía
Santa Isabel 52, Madrid
museoreinasofia.mcu.es
See also: www.spanisharts.com/reinasofia/picasso.htm

Museo Picasso
Montcada 15-23
Ciutat Vella
Parc 08003
Barcelona
www.museupicasso.bcn.es

UNITED KINGDOM
Tate Modern
Bankside
London SE1 9TG
www.tate.org.uk

UNITED STATES
Museum of Modern Art
(Under renovation until 2005.
See web site for further details.)
11 West 53rd Street
New York, NY 10019
www.moma.org

The Guggenheim Museum
1701 5th Avenue
New York, NY
www.guggenheim.org
(web site connects with the four
other Guggenheim museums in
Bilboa, Berlin, Venice, and Las Vegas)

See also:
The Online Picasso Project
A comprehensive study of Picasso with a chronology of his life and useful links to other sites and museums.
www.tamu.edu/mocl/picasso

Index